Alphie the Angel's Little Alphabet Book

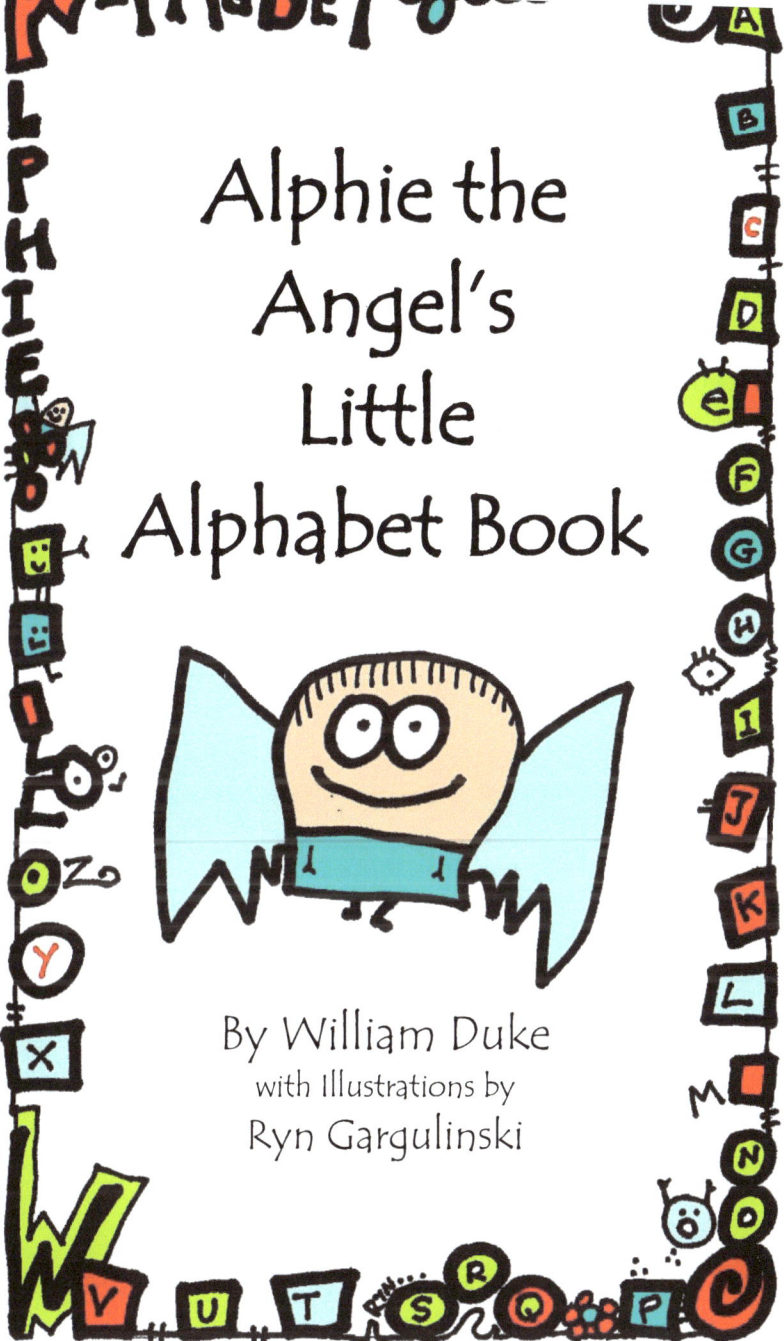

By William Duke

with Illustrations by
Ryn Gargulinski

For More Information:
Contact William Duke
Williamduke153@gmail.com
Ryn Gargulinski
ryngargulinski@hotmail.com

DEDICATION

To my lovely wife
Madonna,
who inspires me
to be a better person.

-William Duke

A

is for
accepting

your wild crazy life,
big tragedies
small annoyances
along with all the
disturbing attributes
of others.

IT IS WHAT IT IS

ACCEPTANCE IS THE ANSWER

B is for being.

Being **beautiful** and **brave**. B is for **becoming better**. B is for **boundaries** to be crossed. B is also for **being** with your breath.

I AM beautiful

C is for **curious.**

C is for **candid,**
avoiding the disguises
that shield us from
others and ourselves.
C is also for **celebrating,**
change and **connection.**

Pow&
WoW

The only constant is
CHANGE..!!

Celebrate...

RYN

D is for
daily

the timeframe for all good
habits that build
a creative life.
D is also for **death**, our
reminder of the short time
we have left.

Create daily for best results.

Rxx...

E is for

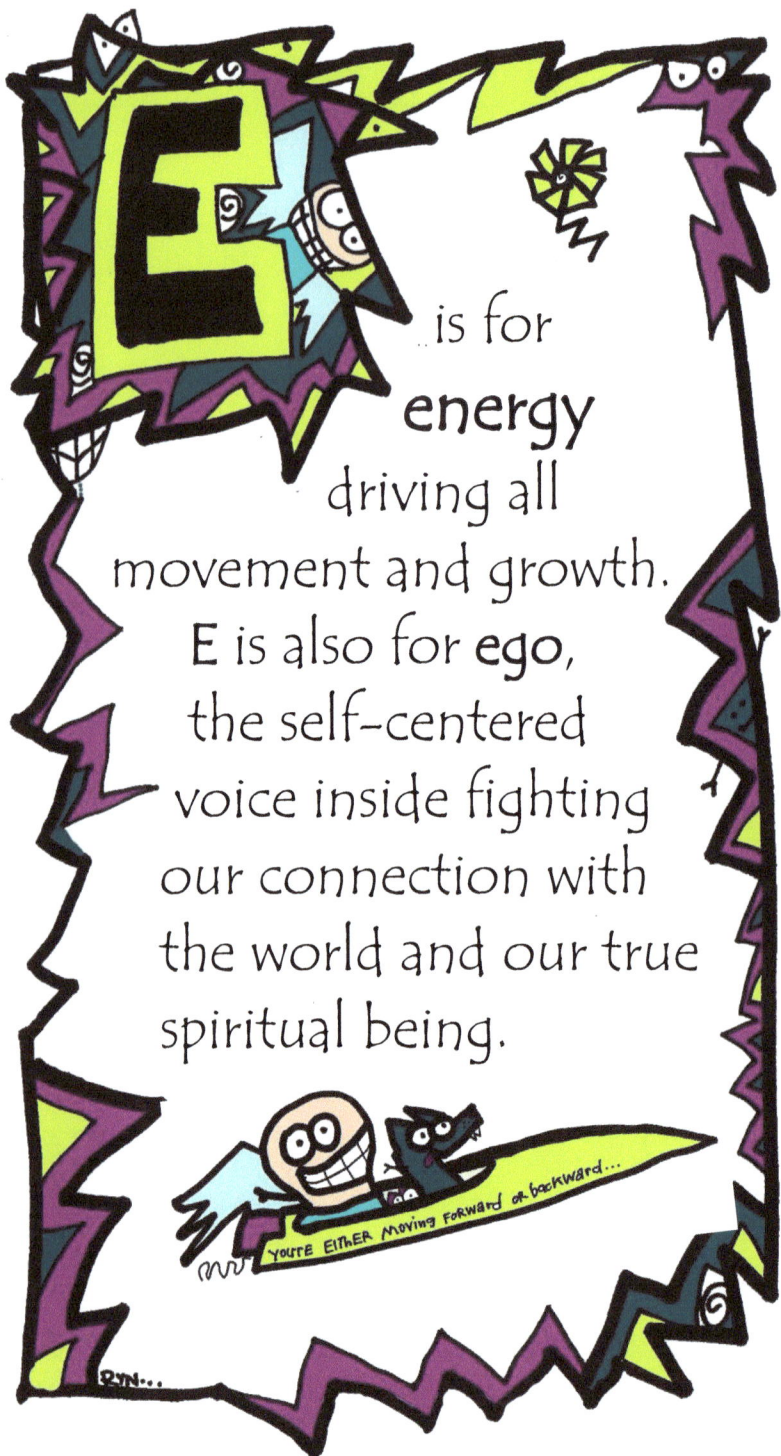

energy
driving all
movement and growth.
E is also for **ego**,
the self-centered
voice inside fighting
our connection with
the world and our true
spiritual being.

YOU'RE EITHER Moving FORWARD OR backward...

F is for **friendship**,

new, lost and enduring. Also **faith** that everything will turn out all right in the end.

ALL'S well that ENDS well.

G is for

gratitude,

the wide lens that is the healthy way to see our large and imperfect world. Also **generosity**. Be **generous** with all things, including your time.

Thank You. Amen.

Thank You.

is for
honesty –
an ideal that allows us to
believe in ourselves and
others. To be honest is
also to be **humble**,
understanding our small
place in the big world.

WE are but a speck of sand...

I is for **integrity,**

a silent, unspoken purity of purpose. Also **intellect,** what's gained by study and questioning. And **intuition,** the little voice inside that lets you know you're on the right path.

YOU'RE ON IT! GO! GO!

J is for
job.

Everyone has a job.
What is yours?

IT'S NOT WORK IF YOU LOVE WHAT YOU DO.

RYN.

K is for **kindness,** the best expression of our humanity to others and ourselves.

...ALL ARE WELCOME

L Is for **love,**

the strong connection between everyone and everything, and the fragrant atmosphere that surrounds us in our highest state.

ALL YOU NEED IS LOVE (and a Dog)

M is for the **moment**

OM

we engage in now.
OM... Also **meditation**,
allowing us to look
objectively at our mind
and our place on the
planet.

YOU ARE HERE

NOW IS THE ONLY MOMENT WE'LL EVER HAVE

RYN:

N

is for **now**,

the ephemeral point always appearing and dissolving into the future.

REJOICE! IN the NOW! It's all we got.....

O

Is for **open.**

Open mind and **open** heart, the vessel that contains love, and serves others, nature and our highest self.

WOW!

...OPEN YOUR Mind: GOOD Things HAPPEN...

P is for

patience,

for enduring
boredom,
failure
and being powerless
over outcomes.

ALL IN GOD'S TIME... TIME...

YOU'RE EXACTLY
WHERE YOU'RE SUPPOSED TO BE.

Q is for

quiet.

THE SWEET SOUND OF SILENCE...

SHHHH

R is for **rest**.

Also **recovery** and keeping it real.

REST . . . . in a Hammock if possible.

RYN . . .

S is for **silence,**

the fertile soil of serenity. Solitude is sacred. S is also for **spirit** and your **spirit guides** who light your way.

Let your intuition guide you...

T is for **transition.**

Death is just another **transition**. We are forever moving through time and different physical states of being. **Trust** this: it is the **truth**.

FOREVER changing...

U is for **understanding** each other and yourself.

You+Me=ONE

RYN

V is for **valor**, or perseverance and fearlessness in the face of adversity. V is also for **vritti**, the whirlpools confusing our thoughts.

You can do it!

RYN..:

W is for **waking,**

waking up to the
beauty of the world
around us.

You FIND WHAT YOU LOOK FOR.

X is for **Xanadu**

the magic city
in our imagination.

OPEN YOUR MIND & You open the door.

Y is for **young,**

keeping a fresh outlook and staying curious in our changing world.

You are as young as you FEEL.

Z is for
the
zone,

Being in the **zone** is
forgetting yourself
and being in the "now."

You are here (always)

www.ingramcontent.com/pod-product-compliance
Lightning Source LLC
Chambersburg PA
CBHW041820040426

42452CB00004B/162